MY FIRST BOOK OF

MADAGASCAR

MADAGASCAR IS THE ONLY PLACE IN THE WORLD WHERE WILD LEMURS LIVE, AS THEY ARE ENDEMIC TO THIS REGION.

LEMURS

MADAGASCAR IS HOME TO SIX SPECIES OF BAOBAB TREES, WITH ONE, THE ADANSONIA BAOBAB, BEING ONE OF THE THICKEST TREES IN THE WORLD.

BAOBABS

MADAGASCAR IS WHERE YOU CAN FIND THE LARGEST CHAMELEON IN THE WORLD - THE ROYAL CHAMELEON - REACHING UP TO 70 CM IN LENGTH.

CHAMELEONS

RAMBUTAN, AN EXOTIC FRUIT RESEMBLING A STAR IN SHAPE, IS ONE OF THE POPULAR FRUITS CULTIVATED IN MADAGASCAR.

RAMBUTAN

PEOPLE IN MADAGASCAR SPEAK MALAGASY, WHICH IS ONE OF THE FEW AUSTRONESIAN LANGUAGES IN AFRICA.

LANGUAGE

MADAGASCAR IS CALLED THE "RHINOCEROS ISLAND" DUE TO ITS DISTINCTIVE RHINOCEROS-SHAPED COASTLINE.

RHINOCEROS

THIS PLACE IN
MADAGASCAR IS
FAMOUS FOR
UNIQUE ROCK
FORMATIONS
CALLED "TSINGY,"
RESEMBLING
NEEDLE-LIKE
BLADES.

TSINGY

ONE OF THE INTERESTING VOLCANOES IN MADAGASCAR IS ANKARATRA, ALSO KNOWN AS THE "GUN BARREL VOLCANO" DUE TO THE SHAPE OF ITS CRATER.

VOLCANOES

MADAGASCAR WAS ONCE HOME TO A SMALL SPECIES OF HIPPOPOTAMUS, WHICH HAS LONG BEEN EXTINCT.

HIPPOPOTAMUS

THE MADAGASCAR FOSSA IS A LARGE CARNIVOROUS HERBIVORE RESEMBLING A CAT, LIVING EXCLUSIVELY IN MADAGASCAR.

FOSSA

MADAGASCAR'S COASTLINE FEATURES BEACHES WITH GOLDEN-COLORED SAND, MAKING THEM UNIQUE AND BEAUTIFUL.

SANDS

MADAGASCAR IS ONE OF THE LARGEST PRODUCERS OF GREEN SAPPHIRES IN THE WORLD.

SAPPHIRES

MAROMOKOTRO MOUNTAIN THIS IS THE HIGHEST PEAK IN MADAGASCAR, REACHING AN ELEVATION OF 2,876 METERS ABOVE SEA LEVEL.

MOUNTAINS

2,876M

SEE ALSO MY OTHER BOOKS :)